SNOWFLAKE BENTLEY

Jacqueline Briggs Martin

Illustrated by Mary Azarian

Houghton Mifflin Harcourt
Boston New York

I would like to thank Ray Miglionico, archivist at the Jericho Historical Society, for sharing his time, access to the Historical Society's documents, and much information about Wilson Bentley. He is a friend to Wilson Bentley and to all who would know more about the "Snowflake Man." —J.B.M.

www.hmhco.com

The text of this book is set in ITC Weidemann.
The illustrations are woodcuts, hand-tinted with watercolors.

[1] Mullett, Mary B., "The Snowflake Man," *American Magazine* 99 (1925), 28–31.
[2] Bentley, W. A., "The Magic Beauty of Snow and Dew," *National Geographic* 43 (1923), 103–12.

Library of Congress Cataloging-in-Publication Data:
Martin, Jacqueline Briggs.
Snowflake Bentley / Jacqueline Briggs Martin; illustrated by Mary Azarian.
p. cm.
Summary: A biography of a self-taught scientist who photographed thousands of individual snowflakes in order to study their unique formations.
1. Snowflakes—Juvenile literature. 2. Nature photography—Juvenile literature.
3. Meteorologists—United States—Biography—Juvenile literature.
4. Photographers—United States—Biography—Juvenile literature.
[1. Bentley, W. A. (Wilson Alwyn), 1865–1931—Juvenile literature.
2. Bentley, W. A. (Wilson Alwyn), 1865–1931. 3. Scientists. 4. Snow.]
I. Azarian, Mary, ill. II. Title.
QC858.B46M37 1998
551.57'841'092—dc21
[B] 97–12458 CIP AC

ISBN: 978-0-395-86162-2 hardcover
ISBN: 978-0-547-24829-5 paperback

Printed in China
SCP 35 34
4500546275

I n the days
when farmers worked with ox and sled
and cut the dark with lantern light,
there lived a boy who loved snow
more than anything else in the world.

Wilson Bentley was born February 9, 1865, on a farm in Jericho, Vermont, between Lake Champlain and Mount Mansfield, in the heart of the "snowbelt," where the annual snowfall is about 120 inches.

Willie Bentley's happiest days were snowstorm days.
He watched snowflakes fall on his mittens,
on the dried grass of Vermont farm fields,

on the dark metal handle of the barn door.
He said snow was as beautiful as butterflies,
or apple blossoms.

He could net butterflies
and show them to his older brother, Charlie.

Willie's mother was his teacher until he was fourteen years old. He attended school for only a few years. "She had a set of encyclopedias," Willie said. "I read them all."

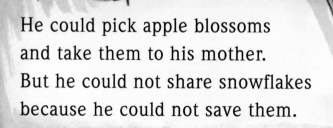

He could pick apple blossoms and take them to his mother. But he could not share snowflakes because he could not save them.

When his mother gave him an old microscope,
he used it to look at flowers, raindrops, and blades of grass.
Best of all, he used it to look at snow.
While other children built forts
and pelted snowballs at roosting crows,
Willie was catching single snowflakes.
Day after stormy day he studied the icy crystals.

From his boyhood on, he studied all forms of moisture. He kept a record of the weather and did many experiments with raindrops.

He learned that most crystals had six branches (though a few had three). For each snowflake the six branches were alike. "I found that snowflakes were masterpieces of design," he said. "No one design was ever repeated. When a snowflake melted . . . just that much beauty was gone, without leaving any record behind."

Their intricate patterns were even more beautiful than he had imagined.

He expected to find whole flakes that were the same, that were copies of each other. But he never did.

Willie decided he must find a way to save snowflakes so others could see their wonderful designs.

For three winters he tried drawing snow crystals. They always melted before he could finish.

Starting at age fifteen he drew a hundred snow crystals each winter for three winters.

When he was sixteen, Willie read of a camera
with its own microscope.
"If I had that camera I could
photograph snowflakes," he told his mother.

Willie's mother knew he would not be happy until
he could share what he had seen.
"Fussing with snow is just foolishness," his father said.
Still, he loved his son.
When Willie was seventeen
his parents spent their savings and bought the camera.

The camera made images on large glass negatives. Its microscope could magnify a tiny crystal from sixty-four to 3,600 times its actual size.

It was taller than a newborn calf,
and cost as much as his father's herd of ten cows.
Willie was sure it was the best of all cameras.

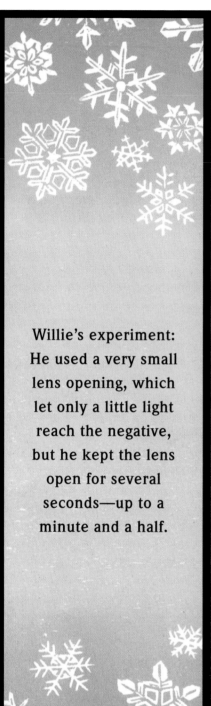

Willie's experiment: He used a very small lens opening, which let only a little light reach the negative, but he kept the lens open for several seconds—up to a minute and a half.

Even so his first pictures were failures—
no better than shadows. Yet he would not quit.
Mistake by mistake, snowflake by snowflake,
Willie worked through every storm.
Winter ended, the snow melted,
and he had no good pictures.
He waited for another season of snow.
One day, in the second winter, he tried
a new experiment. And it worked!
Willie had figured out how to photograph snowflakes!
"Now everyone can see the great beauty
in a tiny crystal," he said.

He learned, too, that he could make the snow crystals show up more clearly by using a sharp knife to cut away all the dark parts of the negative around the crystals. This etching meant extra hours of work for each photograph, but Willie didn't mind.

But in those days no one cared.
Neighbors laughed at the idea of photographing snow.
"Snow in Vermont is as common as dirt," they said.
"We don't need pictures."
Willie said the photographs would be
his gift to the world.

While other farmers sat by the fire or rode to town
with horse and sleigh, Willie studied snowstorms.
He stood at the shed door
and held out a black tray to catch the flakes.

He learned that each snowflake begins as a speck, much too tiny to be seen. Little bits—molecules—of water attach to the speck to form its branches. As the crystal grows, the branches come together and trap small quantities of air. Many things affect the way these crystal branches grow. A little more cold, a bit less wind, or a bit more moisture will mean different-shaped branches. Willie said that was why, in all his pictures, he never found two snowflakes alike.

When he found only jumbled, broken crystals,
he brushed the tray clean with a turkey feather
and held it out again.
He waited hours for just the right crystal
and didn't notice the cold.
If the shed were warm the snow would melt.
If he breathed on the black tray the snow would melt.
If he twitched a muscle as he held the snow crystal
on the long wooden pick the snowflake would break.
He had to work fast or the snowflake would evaporate
before he could slide it into place and take its picture.
Some winters he was able to make only a few dozen
good pictures.
Some winters he made hundreds.

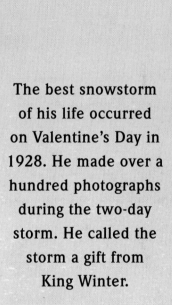

The best snowstorm of his life occurred on Valentine's Day in 1928. He made over a hundred photographs during the two-day storm. He called the storm a gift from King Winter.

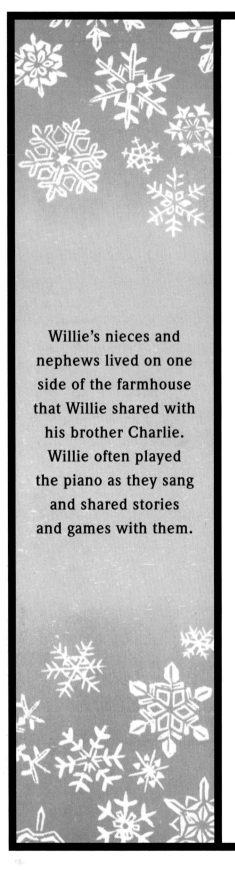

Willie's nieces and nephews lived on one side of the farmhouse that Willie shared with his brother Charlie. Willie often played the piano as they sang and shared stories and games with them.

Willie so loved the beauty of nature
he took pictures in all seasons.
In the summer his nieces and nephews rubbed coat hangers
with sticky pitch from spruce trees.
Then Willie could use them to pick up
spider webs jeweled with water drops and take their pictures.
On fall nights he would gently tie a grasshopper
to a flower so he could find it in the morning
and photograph the dew-covered insect.

But his snow crystal pictures were always his favorites.
He gave copies away or sold them for a few cents.
He made special pictures as gifts for birthdays.
He held evening slide shows on the lawns of his friends.
Children and adults sat on the grass and watched
while Willie projected his slides
onto a sheet hung over a clothesline.

Many colleges and
universities bought
lantern slide copies
of his photographs
and added to their
collections each year.
Artists and designers
used the photographs to
inspire their
own work.

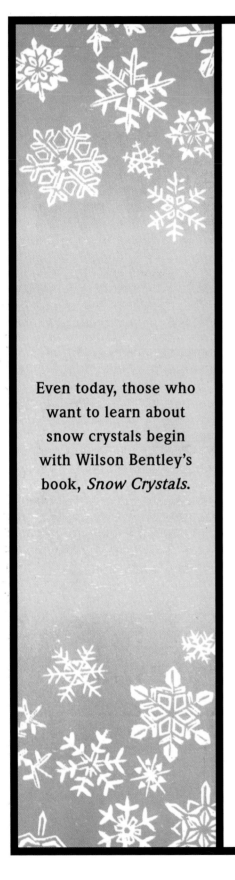

Even today, those who want to learn about snow crystals begin with Wilson Bentley's book, *Snow Crystals*.

He wrote about snow and published his pictures in magazines.
He gave speeches about snow to faraway scholars
and neighborhood skywatchers.
"You are doing a great work," said a professor from Wisconsin.
The little farmer came to be known as
the world's expert on snow, "the Snowflake Man."
But he never grew rich.
He spent every penny on his pictures.
Willie said there were treasures in snow.
"I can't afford to miss a single snowstorm,"
he told a friend. "I never know
when I will find some wonderful prize."
Other scientists raised money so Willie could gather
his best photographs in a book.
When he was sixty-six years old
Willie's book—his gift to the world—was published.
Still, he was not ready to quit.

By 1926 he had spent $15,000 on his work and received $4,000 from the sale of photographs and slides.

Less than a month after
turning the first page on his book,
Willie walked six miles home in a blizzard
to make more pictures.
He became ill with pneumonia after that walk
and died two weeks later.

The plaque on the
monument says

"SNOWFLAKE"
BENTLEY
Jericho's world famous
snowflake authority

For fifty years Wilson A.
Bentley, a simple
farmer, developed his
technique of micro-
photography to reveal to
the world the grandeur
and mystery of the
snowflake—its
universal hexagonal
shape and its infinite
number of lovely
designs.

A monument was built for Willie
in the center of town.
The girls and boys who had been his neighbors
grew up and told their sons and daughters the story
of the man who loved snow.
Forty years after Wilson Bentley's death,
children in his village worked
to set up a museum in honor of the farmer-scientist.
And his book has taken the delicate snow crystals
that once blew across Vermont,
past mountains, over the earth.
Neighbors and strangers
have come to know of the icy wonders
that land on their own mittens—
thanks to Snowflake Bentley.

*"The average dairy farmer gets up at dawn because he has to go to work in the cow yard.
I get up at dawn, too. But it is because I want to find some leaf, hung with dew; or a spider web
which the dew has made into the most delicate ropes of pearls . . . I take my camera with me,
get down on my knees in the wet grass, and photograph these exquisite bits of nature.
Because I do this I can show these lovely things to people who never would have seen them
without my help. They will get their daily quart of milk, all right. Other farmers will attend to that.
But I think I am giving them something which is just as important."*

— *W. A. Bentley*[1]